red flags

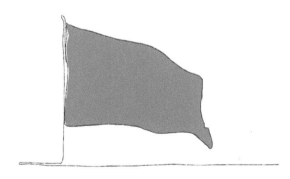

There you stood, my twin flame waving a flag that looked crisp white from a distance.

Each step closer revealed the flag-stained red.

The journey to you was long, but you allowed your battles before me to bleed you dry as the drops blemished your flag.

Your flag wasn't a case of surrender, it was a warning.

-   warning

I didn't invest in myself enough before meeting you.

If I had, our relationship would have soared into beauty instead of crashing into flames.

I knew no boundaries for myself.

I can no longer play victim to being a hopeless romantic.

The universe was just vibrating off my frequency.

Looking for acceptance from people who don't care about you is equivalent to trying to wear a pair of shoes that won't fit. If you keep trying, you're asking for pain, rejection, and wounds bound to open. It comes with sex, empty promises, broken trusts, accusations, and emotional abuse, sometimes physical abuse.

Nothing good comes from it, but sweet spoken words and actions remain absent. "It" does and says just enough to keep you around. For a couple of days or weeks, you are the queen that you indeed are, and then once you are hooked, everything goes back to how it was. "It" refuses to be honest with you. "It" lingers around you for its selfish reasons, which is to drain you of the "it" you possess inside of you. It is that complicated, back-and-forth, inconsistent passion that drives you insane. It causes you to lose yourself by trying to give and give constantly. It takes without considering how you may feel and doesn't think twice about giving.

Excuses, excuses, excuses are all you are stuck with. Questions bat your mind as to whether this person truly cares for you or not. "It" leaves you alone when you need love the most but returns void yet feening for more of your honesty, cares, concerns, and loyalty only to devour you leaving you to feel belittled, not good enough. It doesn't know what it could be, how beautiful it could become. It causes many consequences and confusion when the game is over. It has its repercussions when you love someone who doesn't love themselves.
So you're asking yourselves what is "IT"?

- Inexpensive IT

You can be compatible with someone by trauma too;

it's not always love.

Can we exist any other way?
To not be bonded to one another by the depths of our love and the shallows of our flaws that ever so often escapes us.
Flaws continue to rise as if it were heat, burying our love into a burrowing abyss so deep.
Love becomes so dark, our eyes can't adjust.
Flaws become so hot that it burns us.

We don't spit love, we spit fire.

- two raging dragons dancing in a circle

My light shines bright in my eyes. Eager to love through my light, I surround myself around those who act as if my light is dim. Without doubt, my light begins to flicker. Now I'm the flickering light that needs tightening. I can last for a lifetime, but your attention is on the light that lasts less than 3 months. Sure it shines bright, but it burns quicker, then you're out looking for another.

I guess it's harder to notice that my light only needed a quick turn to the right to last that lifetime that you so desperately needed.

- centennial light

He refused to tell the truth giving me a choice of pills red or blue.

Red is what we know of passion, love, courage, and strength. Taking a look from the lesser end of his choice it's filled with rage, malice, stress, lust, and impulse.

Blue is what we remember to be trusting, stable, loyal, and faithful. When I asked him for the truth expecting a hard pill to swallow of honesty blue, without thought he shoved down my throat the pill of the lesser end of the bloody hue.

The twinkle he left in my eye turned to dust as he wasn't strong enough to resist the yearnings of lust. To honor our love by giving me the blue pill may have been ill, but I wouldn't be at this stand still. Either way it's a lose lose. The greatest ruse I've given myself is knowing you were my muse.

I took you back with ease each time.

It isn't the past humiliation that bothers me, it's knowing I'm still disrespecting myself by still being with you,

   even with forgiveness.

The tears I've cried, this pain that has yet to die. These feelings that I'm feeling aren't even mine. The moment you laid with her, you gave her a portion of our soul tie.

I lost sense of myself, wondering why.

A place in her bed where I'll never physically step, is where my power lies.

I've given my power to people freely without thought.
I left my power in certain places I've lived and once I visited,

I felt helpless.

The problem isn't that she didn't know her worth,

the problem is she was waiting

for them to notice.

It was hard to let go of the fantasy of you,
of us,
which made it harder to actually let go of us.

One look at you and everything was vibrant, everything so beautiful you were made in diamonds. Mesmerized by the image I captured so vividly in my heart, your confession to stop painting you rose gold was becoming so clear, I'd have to restart. You began to tell the truth of the real you and my version of you is incorrect.

You're not rose gold, you are but they're just specks. You show and tell me to look at the real you and once I do, I'll see you'll never be the rose gold painting I created you to be. The more I stopped painting and strip you, my creation, the more I lose you and that's something I cannot face.

I have to strip you down from what I see and realize the real you is someone I can't keep in my place. I keep thinking if I hold on to my version of you, I get to keep my painting.

I have to let you go, see you can't fit into my world, so I release you and pray that one day you actually shine rose gold.

Scrolling through my contacts to find the right call is a substitute from not being able to call you.

I stayed in toxic overdue relationships due to attachment issues. I noticed these attachment issues stemmed from my abandonment issues. While dealing with these abandonment issues, I made an invisible vow to be validated from others. I would always ask myself why can't they see me. It wasn't until I cried and begged my lover "I just want to be seen and heard by you." His reply "I do."

I was seeking validation. I wanted a pat on the back for being the good girlfriend. I wanted a congratulations for completing college and figuring out motherhood with mother and father wounds. I wanted to be saved by someone that loves me the way I love. I loved hard because I yearned to be loved properly by others. Not knowing I had to put in the work to love myself the way I desired.

I'm not his dream girl
I'm the girl of his one-time dream
He tries to chase that same dream like he's trying to find his
first high.

I'm not his ideal girl
I'm the girl he sees and gets a glimpse of a life that is ideal

I'm not the girl he wants
I'm the girl that he wants to need, that itch he scratches for but
can never reach

I'm always three steps ahead, three because one, two steps
give him a chance to touch me and with one more he's caught
up, and once he does, I become a blur.

I'm too close to see for the farsighted that tries to see near.

I'm too right for the guy that's left.
Left behind while chasing fantasies and lust.

Sometimes a person can only see your growth just as much as they have grown.

Understand that there are people who refuse to see you just to make themselves feel better about who they are.

commitments

to self....

this book is a dedication to the reader.

This journey of healing is about you, a time to come back to your authentic self, releasing what no longer serves you. Do not use this sacred time concerning yourself of what others are thinking of you or what he or she is doing with their time.

This is about YOU.

Commitment 1

Romanticize YOUR life.

No one can love you like you. Be your own vibe, be THE innerG you want to attract.

Visualize and realize how beautiful everything in your life already is, how the pain you've endured was the exact chaos you need/needed to discover the true beauty of you.

Widen that tunnel vision just far enough and watch how everything reveals itself. Take yourself on dates, dance, have moments where you talk to yourself in the mirror like Issa. You're not crazy, you're just getting know you.

Make that commitment to yourself and keep it.

I've always frowned upon romance.

I grew fond of romance once I learned to love myself.

Romance is love

    love is liberation

        liberation is what we all crave for and seek.

Commitment 2

There are many types of love and different ways of loving.

love yourself in all of those many types and ways before

loving someone else.

Liberation that is shackled and residing in

darkness becomes the brightest to shine once broken free.

Commitment 3

Living in the present is the bravest act of self-love.

Put all of your being in that moment.

The past doesn't have a hold on you asking to be resolved.

The future isn't asked to be seen or thought of.

The present requires you to trust and love yourself in confidence through any emotion and experience.

Be brave and live in the now.

Commitment 4

REMINDER:

Sleep is luxurious, pamper yourself with rest

Commitment 5

Your energy is your currency.

You have every right to take every part of yourself you gave to others and places back and transform it into something greater.

You break, how you break.

You look inward, prioritize, focus, and improve at your own pace,

HEAL (do not rush the process)

HEAL AGAIN (this is not going to happen in 3 months)

HEAL AGAIN.

Before you know it, you've moved on.

Jealousy housed my lack of confidence.

I had to BURN it down.

I change with the seasons.

I stand out or I choose to blend where I see fit rapidly shifting like a chameleon.

I'm a wanderer that constantly wonders a life of stability, the white picket fence a grand garden in back.

Knowing my life will be filled in awe of boredom trying to get instability back.

Inconsistency is anything but foreign to me, in fact it's paradise.

Why settle for steady when life is all about taking chances and rolling the dice?

Commitment 6

The only validation I seek is from myself.

Commitment 7

AFFIRMATION:

I create space for my personal peace.

Commitment 8

Bare minimum... HA!

what is that?!

Love yourself enough to soar above the bare minimum

Commitment 9

Remember what an honor it is to live your life.

No one can live your life the way you can.

Grasp every moment and feel it.

There's beauty in that moment.

Luxury to me is waking up and living my life at a steady pace. Everything is serene…

> from the music in my background,
>> to the cool water splashing my plush skin.

The cottons and silks that snug my body or hang loosely allowing my body to breathe.

I am the main character of this story that I choose to create on a daily basis.

Commitment 10

Forgive yourself and love yourself gently.

Leaving all known things to elevate is tough.

With elevation, I carry those sweet memories of those nights I wish I can do over. The familiar faces that bring fun and comfort.

Those places I visited where I wish I could have 5 more minutes to just be.
I have to leave a piece of myself to gain a piece of a newer me.

Clearing the path for room for improvement.
Somewhat of Spring cleaning.
Familiar is home that the spirit won't allow me to settle.

I came back to this life as a wanderer always traveling into the unknown.

When I choose the familiar, my life becomes foreign.

When I choose foreign, my life becomes familiar.

Those who choose to explore and elevate are one of the many brave.

Commitment 11

I love myself enough to not torture myself of negative thoughts of the past.
Those thoughts no longer serve me.
I love being in a loving, healthy relationship with myself.

There are three perspectives: the way you view yourself, the way others view you, and who you really are.

Which perspective matters to you?

Choose wisely.

Commitment 12

Instead of complaining,

change it,

release it,

elevate.

Do what you need to do, just don't complain.

You can rewrite your story at any time.

Motherhood Affirmations

I handle one cry at a time.

I handle one mommy at a time.

I handle one expression of one's emotions at a time.

I handle one child at a time.

I pace through motherhood with patience.

I have patience with myself and my emotions

I have patience with my child.

I have patience with my children.

I accept my role in my child's life and their roles in mine.

I accept that I am doing the best I can.

I am learning from my child just as much as I teach them.

I am learning from my children just as much as I teach them.

I am raising my little person the best way I know how.

I am open minded when it comes to parenting.

I am always open to discovering what works for me and my child.

I pace through motherhood with patience.

I am learning myself again.

I am important; I make time for self-care.

I am a priority; my well-being matters.

I love myself.

For those hard days…

Commitment 13

Admire both strengths and weaknesses about yourself.

You are constantly learning both from life experiences which inspires growth.

And that itself is beautiful.

I don't respect the person you were, making it hard to love you in the now.

I've healed too much to still be in love with you as the unhealed me would be.

The you now is asking for a chance, approaching with a fresh start.

A new love.

It is the old you that survives in my head, letting me know that I don't need a new you.
I need to experience something new without you.

Loving myself correctly first will lead me to accepting the correct love for me.

****

My inner masculine won't rest until it knows WE are safe; if you never experience my feminine, you have yourself to blame.

when i accepted you for who you are instead of who i thought
you to be,

i had to love you different and i had to love me more.

I'm uncomfortable in this relationship.

I forgave you.

I thought once forgiveness sat in, I would be comfortable.

I would feel safe.

But somehow discomfort remains, it's eating me alive.

To be here with you, every second, is to leave myself.

I can't concur.

I've become a blur.

Losing myself, no longer to you, but to who I used to be.

I'm not the girl that tolerates disrespect.
I'm not the girl that thinks she can save you.
I'm not the girl that's waiting for you to understand my love language.

I am the woman that leaves at an inch of disrespect.
I am the woman that saves herself.
I am the woman that loves herself and creates languages of love for herself.

This is a me season.

My time is valuable,
my words stand with meaning,
my confidence is on that high horse, that I have don't have to
be loud because my ethereal presence draws in a crowd.

Baby I'm flourishing.

There's no way in hell I can reward your disloyalty by
staying.

I am the greatest love of my life.

I am my own epic love story.

I don't depend on man for an epic tale of true, fantasized love or a romantic love.

I prefer man to be gentle with me, yes. I prefer man to caress me with pleasure, yes. I prefer man to share a story with a time or dozen, yes. Man plays a small part of my love story.

But man does not lie in this skin, man does not take care of this vessel, man does not think my thoughts or train them to say good things to me.

Man does not see my flaws and learn to love them even on those days when loving these flaws aren't linear. Man can love someone else greater than himself or me while lying in me.

I am the great love of this epic tale of romance. The stars of my birth right told me so. Another lifetime ago, I believe I loved man before me. I came back with the same thought, wanting to be loved desperately by he. Until he broke me time and time again, in different bodies, with different laughs and quirks. But each body be familiar spirit. He broke me because I didn't fix me.

I myself am my own love story. My love for me isn't linear either, but it's far greater to give myself the power to love me better than anyone could.

<u>Commitment 14</u>

The many times I've had to mother and celebrate myself,

I'll never again allow someone else to take my power.

Commitment 15

My love for me knows boundaries.

My love for me knows when to walk away.

My love for me knows any hurt from others does not begin with me, but with them.

My love for me has no room for victim mentality.

My love for me pushes fear out.

My love for me only allows those who make me feel good in honor of my space.

My love for me will never bring me harm, only peace.

Negative projection from them requires major protection for you.

Commitment 16

REMINDER:

Don't repeat that toxic cycle because you're bored. You're wanting to look back because it's familiar and somewhat a safety net.

You're doing great by moving forward.

Keep going.

Commitment 17

REMINDER:

On the brink of elevation, you may begin to miss the familiar.

The familiar is safe, but the unknown has greater in store.
Keep pushing yourself out of your comfort zone.

You got this.

Commitment 18

Slow down. Love slow. I've always loved fast, being afraid that if i didn't love fast enough they would speed off.

I learn to take things slow. Pace easily with everything.

Everything that is for me, is already mine.

Rest, Reset, Reflection

The goal is growth.

You are allowed to become a better, different version of yourself.

About the Author

Jennifer Harris is a teacher and advocate for mental health awareness and self love. Her previous works include *Unraveling* (2021) and *What About Me?!!* (2019). *Unraveling* brings awareness of healing by recognition of trauma, seeking help, and being able to work through those issues of grief through affirmations. Her children's book, *What About Me?!!* is to help both adults and children learn to adjust to a new member of the family as their worlds are turned upside down. She is currently working on a series entitled *Oh, Joy,* a love letter to growth and self-love for children. *Oh, Joy* is available on Kindle Vella with episodes revealed weekly. *DAWN,* her spoken word EP, is available on all platforms.

Instagram: @jenuinepoetry   Website: linkt.ree/jenuinepoetry

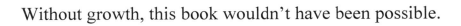

Without growth, this book wouldn't have been possible.

Lightning Source UK Ltd.
Milton Keynes UK
UKHW021516100223
416667UK00011B/475

9 781087 983202